Five-Minute
SUNDAY SCHOOL
ACTIVITIES

JESUS' MiRACLES
AND MESSAGES

Rainbow Publishers

Rainbow Publishers • P.O. Box 70130 • Richmond, VA 23255
www.rainbowpublishers.com

Five-Minute

Sunday School Activities

Jesus' Miracles and Messages

Mary J. Davis

To my husband Larry, our children and their families.
To Judy, Bona Dean and Grandma May: family by chance, friends by choice.

FIVE-MINUTE SUNDAY SCHOOL ACTIVITIES: JESUS' MIRACLES AND MESSAGES
©2006 by Rainbow Publishers, third printing
ISBN 10: 1-58411-049-X
ISBN 13: 978-1-58411-049-1
Rainbow reorder# RB38422
church and ministry/ministry resources/children's ministry

Rainbow Publishers
P.O. Box 70130
Richmond, VA 23255
www.rainbowpublishers.com

Interior Illustrator: Chuck Galey
Cover Illustrator: Todd Marsh

Scriptures are from the *Holy Bible: New International Version* (North American Edition), ©1973, 1978, 1984 by the International Bible Society. Used by permission of Zondervan Bible Publishers.

Printed in the United States of America

CONTENTS

INTRODUCTION

Children need to grow up learning about Jesus. God's Word will teach elementary children about Jesus' love and care for us. Jesus' parables and miracles are wonderful teaching tools. Children will understand that Jesus cares, Jesus loves, and Jesus wants them to know about God and heaven.

Five-Minute Sunday School Activities is designed to give teachers a quick activity that teaches an important Bible truth. Teachers are often faced with a few extra minutes after the lesson is finished. There are also times when a teacher needs a few moments to get attendance and other important matters out of the way before the main lesson. Instead of wasting these minutes with non-learning play, provide a *Five-Minute* activity!

The activities in the book can also be used as entire lessons. Bible story references, teaching suggestions, and memory verses are included with each activity.

EXTRA TIME suggestions are given for each activity. If you have more than five minutes, extend the lesson time with the **EXTRA TIME** option.

THE SOWER AND THE SEED
MARK 4:3-20

WHAT YOU NEED

- page 12, duplicated
- markers or crayons
- pencils

BEFORE CLASS

Duplicate a pattern page for each child.
Make a sample craft to show the children.

WHAT TO DO

1. Introduce the lesson by telling the parable from Mark 4:3-20. Discuss what the verse means: when people hear the Word of God, they tell others and then those people tell others and so on. Say, **We help the church to grow when we share about God with others.**
2. Show the children the sample craft.
3. Distribute a pattern page to each child.
4. Have the children color both pictures as they wish. While the children work, recite the memory verse with them a few times.
5. Have the children take turns reading the following pairs of verses aloud from Mark 4 so they may understand the lesson better: 4 and 15, 5-6 and 16-17, 7 and 18-19, 8 and 20. Ask, **How can we be more like the seed sown on good soil?**
6. On the lines above the people worshiping in church, have the children write the names of people they can tell about God.

EXTRA TIME

Play "Tell Somebody." Arrange the class in a circle. Start by giving one child a Bible. Have the student hold the Bible and tell or read his or her favorite Bible story. Then that child should pass the Bible to the next child. Continue until each child has read or told a short Bible story (prompt those who have trouble coming up with an idea by suggesting stories). Remind the children that God wants us to share His Word with others and help the church to grow.

Can you be a sower in God's garden? Write names of people you will tell about God on the lines below.

Others, like seed sown on good soil, hear the word, accept it, and produce a crop.

~ Mark 4:20

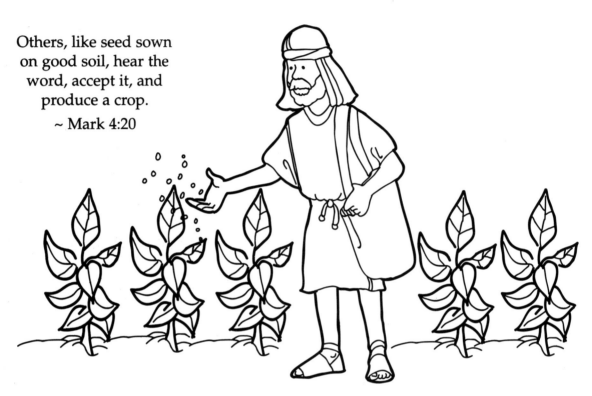

NEW WINE IN OLD WINESKINS
MATTHEW 9:14-17

MEMORY VERSE

*They pour new wine into new wineskins,
and both are preserved.*

~ Matthew 9:17

WHAT YOU NEED

- page 14, duplicated
- pencils

BEFORE CLASS

Duplicate a pattern page for each child.

WHAT TO DO

1. Introduce the lesson by telling the parable in Matthew 9:14-17. Say, **Jesus was trying to help others understand that He came to be a witness about God and heaven. He wanted everyone around Him to think about God's work, which is the most important thing.**
2. Distribute a pattern page to each child.
3. Say the memory verse.
4. Tell the children to solve the puzzle by looking at the key and filling in the blank spaces with the correct vowels. Add to the lesson by having the children write out Matthew 9:16 on the back of the activity page. Say, **Jesus brought new ways into the world. He wanted us to know His ways were new and that they were different from some of the Old Testament ways.**

EXTRA TIME

Play Tug of War. Provide three or four towels. Have the children use plastic yarn needles and yarn to sew the towels together in a long strip (or you may want to do the sewing before class). Divide the class into two teams. Have a tug of war with the sewn towels. When the towels tear apart, remind the children of the lesson theme.

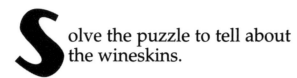

S olve the puzzle to tell about the wineskins.

Key

▲ = a

● = e

■ = i

❙ = o

◗ = u

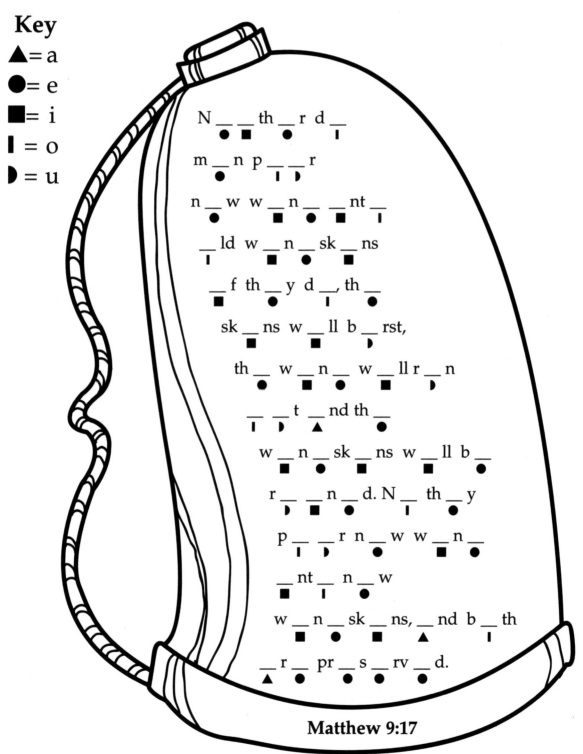

N _ _ th _ r d _
  ● ■   ●   ❙

m _ n p _ _ r
  ●   ❙ ◗

n _ w w _ n _ _ nt _
  ●   ■ ● ■   ❙

_ ld w _ n _ sk _ ns
❙   ■ ●   ■

_ f th _ y d _, th _
■   ●   ❙   ●

sk _ ns w _ ll b _ rst,
  ■   ■   ◗

th _ w _ n _ w _ ll r _ n
  ●   ■ ●   ■   ◗

_ _ t _ nd th _
❙ ◗   ▲   ●

w _ n _ sk _ ns w _ ll b _
 ■ ●   ■   ■   ●

r _ _ n _ d. N _ th _ y
 ◗ ■ ●   ❙   ●

p _ _ r n _ w w _ n _
 ❙ ◗   ●   ■ ●

_ nt _ n _ w
■   ❙ ●

w _ n _ sk _ ns, _ nd b _ th
 ■ ●   ■   ▲   ❙

_ r _ pr _ s _ rv _ d.
▲ ●   ● ●   ●

Matthew 9:17

The solution is on page 95.

THE WEEDS

MATTHEW 13:24-30, 36-43

WHAT YOU NEED

- page 16, duplicated
- crayons or markers
- pencils
- yarn
- tape

BEFORE CLASS

Duplicate a pattern page for each child. Make a sample craft to show the children.

WHAT TO DO

1. Introduce the lesson by telling the story from Matthew 13:24-30, 36-43. Ask, **What will happen to everything that causes sin? What will happen to those who do evil? How will God take care of His righteous people?**
2. Show the children the sample craft.
3. Distribute a pattern page to each child.
4. Say the memory verse.
5. Tell the children to write out Matthew 13:41 on the lines of the barn.
6. Have the children color the plaque as time allows. Discuss things that cause sin and evil (lying, stealing, disobedience, etc.).
7. Show how to tape a yarn loop to the top of the barn for a hanger.

EXTRA TIME

Make a Parable Mobile. Have the children glue the page to red construction paper, then cut out the barn shape. Have the children cut out a circle from yellow construction paper to represent the sun. Tell the children to write Matthew 13:43 (see below) on the sun. Show how to attach a loop of yarn at the top of the barn for hanging and a 4-inch length of yarn at the bottom of the yarn. Instruct the students to tape the sun to the yarn. Verse: "Then the righteous will shine like the sun in the kingdom of their Father" (Matthew 13:43).

ake a verse plaque to remember what will happen to sin and evil.

THE MUSTARD SEED

LUKE 13:18-19

MEMORY VERSE

It is like a mustard seed, which a man took and planted in his garden. It grew and became a tree, and the birds of the air perched in its branches.

~ Luke 13:19

WHAT YOU NEED

- page 18, duplicated
- crayons or markers
- scissors
- mustard seeds
- yarn
- glue

BEFORE CLASS

Duplicate a pattern page for each child. Make a sample craft to show the children.

WHAT TO DO

1. Introduce the lesson by having the children take turns reading the parable from Luke 13:18-19. Show some small seeds and pictures of trees or large plants. Say, **Jesus wants us to know that the kingdom of heaven is better than we could imagine.**
2. Show the children the sample craft.
3. Distribute a pattern page to each child.
4. Say the memory verse.
5. Have the children cut out the pendant. Each child should also cut 2 to 3 feet of yarn.
6. Show how to fold the pendant over the yarn and glue the two sides of the pendant together, then tie the yarn ends together.
7. Have the children glue a mustard seed onto the pendant, then color it as time allows.

EXTRA TIME

Provide old magazines, seeds and glue. Have the children work together to make a mural. Instruct them to cut out pictures of trees, large plants and birds from the magazines. Show how to glue the pictures and seeds onto a large piece of poster paper or a bulletin board. Write the memory verse across the top of the mural.

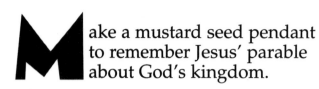

Make a mustard seed pendant to remember Jesus' parable about God's kingdom.

It is like a mustard seed, which a man took and planted in his garden. It grew and became a tree, and the birds of the air perched in its branches.
Luke 13:19

The kingdom of heaven...

is like a mustard seed.

THE LOST SHEEP
LUKE 15:3-7

MEMORY VERSE

I tell you that in the same way there will be more rejoicing in heaven over one sinner who repents than over ninety-nine righteous persons who do not need to repent.

~ Luke 15:7

I tell you that in the same way there will be more rejoicing in heaven over one sinner who repents than over ninety-nine righteous persons who do not need to repent.
~ Luke 15:7

WHAT YOU NEED

- page 22, duplicated
- crayons or markers
- instant camera

BEFORE CLASS

Duplicate a pattern page for each child. Make a sample craft to show the children.

WHAT TO DO

1. Introduce the lesson by telling the story of the lost sheep from Luke 15:3-7. Say, **This parable tells how much one soul means to God. Each of us is so special to God! The kingdom of heaven rejoices when we repent and become children of God.**
2. Show the children the sample craft.
3. Distribute a pattern page to each child.
4. Say the memory verse.
5. Tell the children to draw a picture of a sheep in the shepherd's arms. Have the children color the picture as time allows.
6. Say, **As in the picture, we are sheep and Jesus is our Good Shepherd. We are precious to Him.**

EXTRA TIME

Have a rejoicing party! Provide musical items such as bells, sticks, small drums and so on. Say the name of each child. After you say each name, have the children make praise to God for that child's dedication to Him.

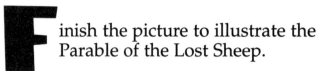

Finish the picture to illustrate the
Parable of the Lost Sheep.

I tell you that in the
same way there will be
more rejoicing in heaven
over one sinner who
repents than over
ninety-nine righteous
persons who do not
need to repent.

~ Luke 15:7

THE UNMERCIFUL SERVANT
MATTHEW 18:23-35

WHAT YOU NEED

- page 24, duplicated
- crayons or markers
- scissors
- tape
- yarn
- plastic drinking straws or craft sticks
- glue
- glitter or colored sand

BEFORE CLASS

Duplicate a pattern page for each child. You will need one 1-foot length of yarn and one straw or craft stick per child. Make a sample craft to show the children.

WHAT TO DO

1. Introduce the lesson by telling the story from Matthew 18:23-35. Discuss times when the children have had to forgive someone or when they needed forgiveness. Ask, **What does God expect you to do when someone has made you angry?**
2. Show the children the sample craft.
3. Distribute a pattern page to each child, and say the memory verse.
4. Have the children cut apart the page on the solid line.
5. Show how to fit the two strips into a long strip and tape them together.
6. Have the children attach a straw to the top of the strip by rolling the top edge of the paper over the straw and taping securely.
7. Show how to thread a length of yarn through the straw, then tie the yarn at the ends for a hanger.
8. Have the children line the letters of FORGIVE with glue, then sprinkle on glitter or colored sand. Remind the children to forgive others.

EXTRA TIME

Provide quarter-sheets of paper and markers. Have the children make coupons that say "Debt Cancelled." Encourage the children to use the coupons when they need to remember to forgive others.

ake a forgiveness banner to show
that God expects us to forgive
others as he forgives us.

F
O
R

G
I
V
E

THE TWO SONS
MATTHEW 21:28-32

REPENT
BELIEVE
SERVE

Matthew 21:28-32

WHAT YOU NEED

- page 26, duplicated
- crayons or markers
- pencils
- scissors

BEFORE CLASS

Duplicate a pattern page for each child. Make a sample craft to show the children.

WHAT TO DO

1. Introduce the lesson by telling the story from Matthew 21:28-32. Say, **God wants us to serve Him, just as the father wanted his sons to work in the vineyard. Can you guess what the vineyard means today? Yes, it is the world. God needs workers to help people know Him. God also wants us to believe in Him, ask Him for forgiveness and serve Him.**
2. Show the children the sample craft.
3. Distribute a pattern page to each child.
4. Say the memory verse.
5. Have the children cut out the folding hand and fold it on the dashed line.
6. On the inside, have the children write: "Yes, Lord, I will." Also, have them sign their name as a promise. Say, **Let's remember our promises and do our best to serve God.**

EXTRA TIME

Plan a project together that can be completed during classtime. The project can be anything to serve God. Some suggestions: clean an area of the church, fold newsletters for mailing or write thank-you notes to church staff.

ake a promise hand. Promise God
that you will serve him as He asks.

THE WEDDING BANQUET
MATTHEW 22:1-4

AN INVITATION

MEMORY VERSE

For many are invited, but few are chosen.
~ Matthew 22:14

WHAT YOU NEED

- page 28, duplicated
- crayons or markers
- pencils

BEFORE CLASS

Duplicate a pattern page for each child.
Make a sample craft to show the children.

WHAT TO DO

1. Introduce the lesson by telling the story from Matthew 22:1-4. Discuss the concept of "chosen." Help the children understand that God wants each of us to accept His invitation, but some people refuse.
2. Show the children the sample craft.
3. Distribute a pattern page to each child.
4. Say the memory verse.
5. Have the children fold the page in half.
6. Encourage the students to write an invitation on the inside of the folded page. Say, **Write an invitation to tell someone that he or she is invited to become a child of God.**
7. Have the children color the front of the invitation as time allows.

EXTRA TIME

Have the class make enough invitations to distribute to another class.

 Make an invitation that tells someone
how to become a child of God.

AN INVITATION

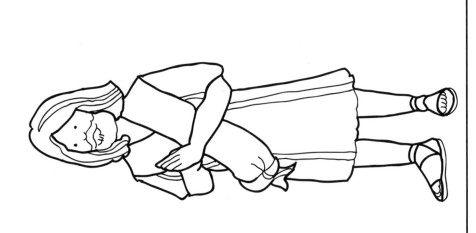

For many are invited, but few are chosen.
~ Matthew 22:14

THE FiG TREE
MARK 13:28-31

MEMORY VERSE

Heaven and earth will pass away, but my words will never pass away.

~ Mark 13:31

WHAT YOU NEED

- page 30, duplicated
- heavy white paper or card stock
- crayons or markers
- scissors
- raffia or ribbon
- clear, self-stick plastic
- hole punch

BEFORE CLASS

Duplicate a pattern page onto heavy white paper or card stock for each child. Make a sample craft to show the children.

WHAT TO DO

1. Introduce the lesson by having the children take turns reading the story from Mark 13:28-31. Discuss some ways today's world tempts us to do things differently than God's Word says.
2. Show the children the sample craft.
3. Distribute a pattern page to each child.
4. Say the memory verse.
5. Have the children cut out and color the two bookmarks.
6. Provide a piece of clear self-adhesive plastic, large enough to cover the front of each bookmark. Help the children apply the plastic to the bookmarks.
7. Help the children punch a hole at the top of each bookmark and tie some raffia or ribbon through the hole.

EXTRA TIME

Make a God's Word Tree to share with other classes or the entire church. Provide a large branch anchored inside a bucket or coffee can with plaster. Have the children write their favorite memory verses on green leaf shapes. Tape the leaves to the tree. Add a sign with the memory verse above to the top of the tree. Display the tree for others to enjoy!

Make Bible bookmarks, one to keep and one to share with someone.

Holy
Bible

Heaven
and
earth
will
pass
away,
but
my
words
will
never
pass
away.

Mark 13:31

Holy
Bible

Heaven
and
earth
will
pass
away,
but
my
words
will
never
pass
away.

Mark 13:31

THe SHeeP aND THe GOaTS

MaTTHew 25:31-46

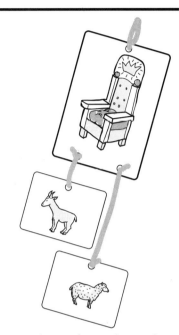

MEMORY VERSE

Then the King will say to those on his right,
"Come, you who are blessed by my Father; take
your inheritance, the kingdom prepared for
you since the creation of the world.

~ Matthew 25:34

WHAT YOU NEED

- page 32, duplicated
- crayons or markers
- scissors
- yarn
- tape

BEFORE CLASS

Duplicate a pattern page for each child. Make a sample craft to show the children.

WHAT TO DO

1. Introduce the lesson by telling the parable from Matthew 25:31-46. Discuss how much God must love each of us to prepare such a beautiful kingdom for us.
2. Show the children the sample craft.
3. Distribute a pattern page to each child, and say the memory verse.
4. Have the children cut out and color the three mobile pieces.
5. Help the children cut three lengths of yarn, around 6 inches long each.
6. Show how to make a loop of yarn with one length and tape it to the top of the throne figure for a hanger.
7. Have the students tape the remaining two straight lengths of yarn to the bottom of the throne figure.
8. Finally, they should tape the sheep figure to the bottom end of one length of yarn, and the goat figure to the bottom of the other. Have the children read Matthew 25:34-46. Ask, **In what ways can we show that we are God's lambs?**

EXTRA TIME

Reproduce and cut out several sheep and goats. Hide the sheep and goats around the room. Let the children look for the sheep and goats. Then gather the children together and let each one tell about a time when he or she helped someone to please God. Say, **God wants us to think about ways we can help others every day. We should make helping others a habit!**

ake a mobile to remember the story of the sheep and goats as Jesus told it.

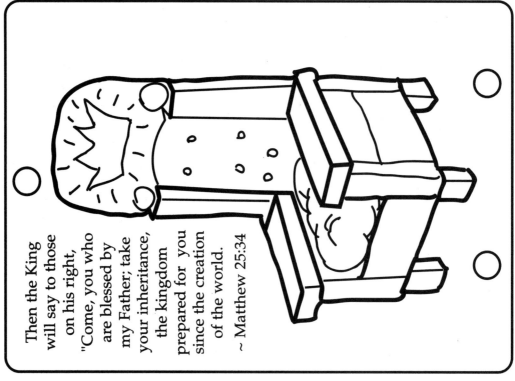

Then the King will say to those on his right, "Come, you who are blessed by my Father; take your inheritance, the kingdom prepared for you since the creation of the world. ~ Matthew 25:34

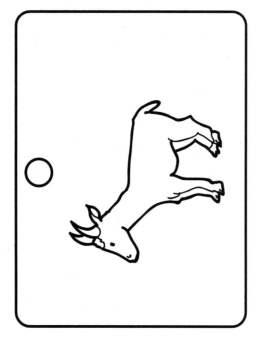

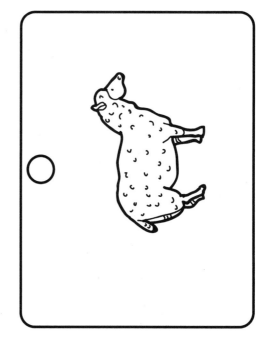

THE RICH FOOL

LUKE 12:16-21

MEMORY VERSE

"This is how it will be with anyone who stores up things for himself but is not rich toward God."

~ Luke 12:21

WHAT YOU NEED

- page 38, duplicated
- pencils

BEFORE CLASS

Duplicate a pattern page for each child. Make a sample craft to show the children.

My Un-greedy Calendar

Monday	Tuesday
SHARED DESSERT WITH SISTER.	LET NATHAN PLAY WITH MY COMPUTER
Wednesday GAVE KYLE 50¢ FOR MILK AT SCHOOL	**Thursday**
Friday	**Saturday**

WHAT TO DO

1. Introduce the lesson by telling the story from Luke 12:16-21. Say, **The rich man was greedy with his grain. But the man's greed made God angry. God doesn't want us to be greedy.**
2. Show the children the sample craft.
3. Distribute a pattern page to each child.
4. Say the memory verse.
5. Talk about being un-greedy. On the back of the page, have the children write some ways to be un-greedy.
6. Encourage the children to use the calendar to write down ways that they are un-greedy.

EXTRA TIME

Play the Un-Greedy Game. Put some treats in plastic sandwich bags (use a variety). Place a bag at each child's place at the table. Instruct the children not to open the bags. During the lesson, occasionally ring a bell. Every time the bell rings, the children should pass their treat bags in different ways (one space over, until the bell rings again, and so on). Say, **Some treats might be your favorites. But it is good to share what we have.**

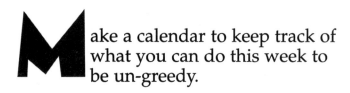

ake a calendar to keep track of what you can do this week to be un-greedy.

My Un-greedy Calendar

Luke 12:16-21

Monday	Tuesday
Wednesday	**Thursday**
Friday	**Saturday**

THE LOST SON

LUKE 15:11-32

Five Minute

MEMORY VERSE

For this son of mine was dead and is alive again; he was lost and is found.

~ Luke 15:24

WHAT YOU NEED

- page 42, duplicated
- crayons or markers
- tape
- paper towel tubes

BEFORE CLASS

Duplicate a pattern page for each child. You will need one paper towel tube per child. Make a sample craft to show the children.

WHAT TO DO

1. Introduce the lesson by telling the parable from Luke 15:11-32. Say, **The father rejoiced that his son returned. God rejoices when a sinner repents and returns to God's way. We should also celebrate when someone we know repents and becomes a child of God.**
2. Show the children the sample craft.
3. Distribute a pattern page to each child.
4. Say the memory verse.
5. Distribute a paper towel tube to each child.
6. Have the children color the pattern, then wrap it around the towel tube.
7. Show how to tape the seams at the "overlap" area. Spend some time praising God. Let the children sing, hum or shout praises.

EXTRA TIME

Play the Winner Game. Place a slip of paper with each child's name on it in a bowl or box. Arrange the class in a circle, standing. Have the children pass around the bowl or box quickly. Shout "stop" now and then. The child holding the bowl or box should draw out a name. The person whose name is called should step into the circle. Have the class say good things to "welcome" the child "home." Repeat the game as long as time allows.

 ake a praise horn to celebrate the return of a lost sinner.

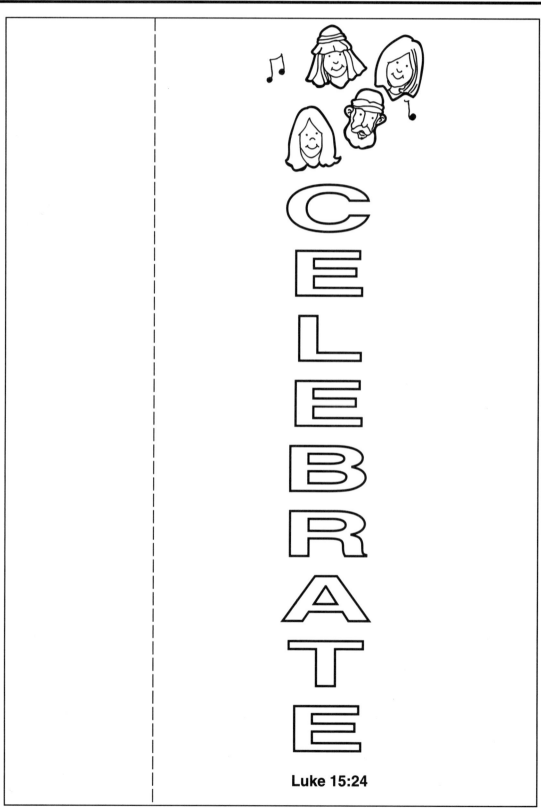

Luke 15:24

THe GROWiNG seeD
MaRK 4:26-29

MEMORY VERSE

Night and day, whether he sleeps or gets up, the seed sprouts and grows, though he does not know how.

~ Mark 4:27

WHAT YOU NEED

- page 44, duplicated
- crayons or markers
- scissors
- tape
- small plastic containers
- soil
- plant seeds

BEFORE CLASS

Duplicate a pattern page for each child. You will need two washed plastic containers per child (margarine, cottage cheese or sour cream containers work well). Make a sample craft to show the children. Option: Provide filled pots so the children can quickly finish the flower pot and plant some seeds in the soil.

WHAT TO DO

1. Introduce the lesson by telling the parable from Mark 4:26-29. Show a live plant. Ask, **Can you see the plant grow? Do plants stop growing when you turn away or go to sleep? The seeds of faith God plants in people grow just like these plants.**
2. Show the children the sample craft.
3. Distribute a pattern page to each child, and say the memory verse.
4. Have the children cut the page apart on the solid line.
5. While the children color the two strips, retell the story.
6. Have the children wrap a strip around each plastic container and tape the seams.
7. Allow the children to fill their containers with soil.
8. Show how to carefully plant the seeds in the soil. Remind the children to use opportunities to plant seeds of faith in others. Ask, **How can we plant seeds of faith in people who need to know God?**

EXTRA TIME

Divide the class into small groups. Have the groups practice ways of planting seeds of faith. Then have the groups act out their ideas for the class.

ake two planters to remember the parable of the growing seed.

Night and day, whether he sleeps or gets up, the seed sprouts and grows, though he does not know how.
Mark 4:27

Night and day, whether he sleeps or gets up, the seed sprouts and grows, though he does not know how.
Mark 4:27

44

THE PHARISEE & TAX COLLECTOR
LUKE 18:9-14

MEMORY VERSE

For everyone who exalts himself will be humbled, and he who humbles himself will be exalted.

~ Luke 18:14

WHAT YOU NEED

- page 50, duplicated
- crayons or markers
- hole punch
- yarn

BEFORE CLASS

Duplicate a pattern page for each child. Make a sample craft to show the children.

WHAT TO DO

1. Introduce the lesson by telling the parable from Luke 18:9-14. Say, **Can you imagine how silly the Pharisee seemed when he prayed about how good he was? God wants us to be sincere, humble and truthful when we pray.**
2. Show the children the sample craft.
3. Distribute a pattern page to each child.
4. Say the memory verse.
5. Have the children fold the page on the solid line, then punch a hole at top.
6. Show how to thread a length of yarn through the hole and tie at the ends for a hanger.
7. On one side, have the children write ways they act proud sometimes. On the other, have them write ways they can be humble.
8. Allow the children to color the plaque as time allows. Have some children read what they listed for pride, then for humble.

EXTRA TIME

Play Proud and Humble Freeze Tag. The child who is It should tag someone and shout either "proud" or "humble." The tagged person then must pose as a proud or humble person. After all the children are tagged, choose another It and play again. Say, **See how silly we look when we try to be proud instead of humble?**

Learn how Jesus says not to pray. Make a plaque to remember to be humble, and not proud.

Write ways you can be like this man (humble).

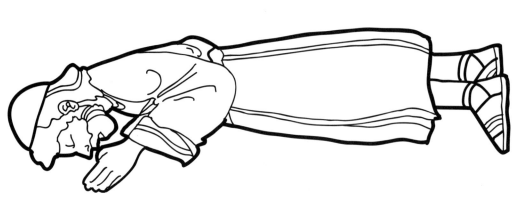

But the tax collector stood at a distance. He said, "God have mercy on me, a sinner." ~ Luke 18:13

Write some ways you might act like this man (proud).

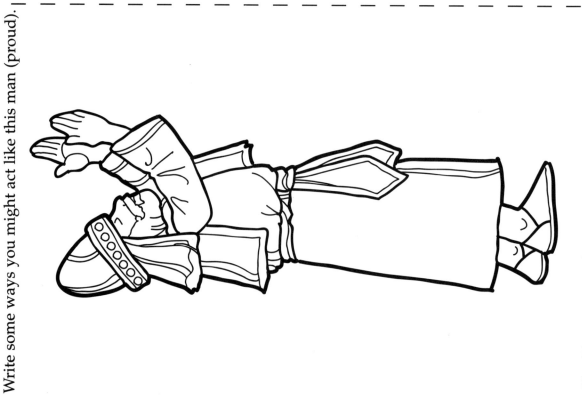

The Pharisee stood up and prayed about himself. ~ Luke 18:11

JESUS TAUGHT THE PEOPLE
MARK 4:1-2

MEMORY VERSE

He taught them many things by parables.
~ Mark 4:2

WHAT YOU NEED

- page 52, duplicated
- crayons or markers
- scissors
- tape
- yarn

BEFORE CLASS

Duplicate a pattern page for each child. Make a sample craft to show the children.

WHAT TO DO

1. Introduce the lesson by having the children take turns reading Mark 4:1-2. Say, **Jesus taught the people about the kingdom of God and how to live like a child of God. We can read these stories in our Bibles and learn these same things.**
2. Show the children the sample craft.
3. Distribute a pattern page to each child.
4. Say the memory verse.
5. Have the children cut out the picture on the solid lines.
6. Show how to roll the edges toward the center by wrapping the paper around a pencil.
7. Have the children color the picture as time allows.
8. Allow the children to attach a loop of yarn to the top with tape for hanging. Say, **The picture will remind you that Jesus taught the people Himself. He wanted them to learn about the kingdom of God, and He wants us to learn, too.**

EXTRA TIME

Have the children take turns telling their favorite Bible stories to the class.

Make a rolled-edge picture to remember that Jesus taught the people. These stories are in our Bibles, and we can learn from them today.

He taught them many things by parables.
Mark 4:2

JESUS TURNS WATER TO WINE

JOHN 2:1-11

MEMORY VERSE

This, the first of his miraculous signs, Jesus performed at Cana in Galilee. He thus revealed his glory, and his disciples put their faith in him.

~ John 2:11

WHAT YOU NEED

- page 54, duplicated
- crayons or markers

BEFORE CLASS

Duplicate a pattern page for each child.

WHAT TO DO

1. Introduce the lesson by telling the story from John 2:1-11. Say, **Not only did Jesus know He had the power of God to do miracles, but His mother, Mary, knew also. After this miracle, those following Jesus knew He was going to do wonderful things to show he was indeed God's Son.**
2. Distribute a pattern page for each child.
3. Say the memory verse.
4. Instruct the children to connect the dots to find out what Jesus told the men to do.
5. Allow the children to color the picture as time permits. Say, **This miracle wasn't just an accidental thing. God had a plan for Jesus' life. Everything was meant to glorify God.**

EXTRA TIME

Have the students turn over the puzzle and write a poem to thank Jesus for His wonderful works.

Follow the dots to discover what Jesus had the men do when the wine ran out.

This, the first of his miraculous signs, Jesus performed at Cana in Galilee.
He thus revealed his glory, and his disciples put their faith in him.

~ John 2:11

The solution is on page 95.

JESUS MAKES A GREAT CATCH

LUKE 5:1-11

MEMORY VERSE

They pulled their boats up on shore, left everything and followed him.

~ Luke 5:11

WHAT YOU NEED

- page 56, duplicated
- crayons or markers

BEFORE CLASS

Duplicate a puzzle for each child.

WHAT TO DO

1. Introduce the lesson by telling the story from Luke 5:1-11. Have the children take turns reading verses 8-11. Say, **When people saw the wonderful things Jesus did, they knew He was from God. The miracles Jesus did helped people have faith in Him.**
2. Distribute a puzzle to each child.
3. Say the memory verse.
4. Encourage the children to find and circle 18 fish in the picture.
5. Have the children color the picture as time allows.

EXTRA TIME

Make a "net full of love" bulletin board. Begin with a background of blue paper. Fasten a net (or opened produce bags that look like a net) onto the bulletin board. Have the children cut out fish shapes from construction paper. Say, **Let's write some blessings we have received.** Write one blessing on each fish. When the children have written on several fish, fasten the fish to the bulletin board. Write "Net Full of Love" on a piece of construction paper as a header for the board.

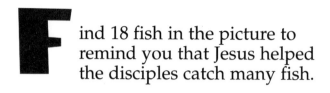

ind 18 fish in the picture to remind you that Jesus helped the disciples catch many fish.

They pulled their boats up on shore, left everything and followed him.

~ Luke 5:11

The solution is on page 95.

Jesus Calms a Storm

Mark 4:35-41

MEMORY VERSE

Even the wind and the waves obey him!
~ Mark 4:41

WHAT YOU NEED

- page 58, duplicated
- heavy paper or card stock
- scissors
- yarn
- tape

BEFORE CLASS

Duplicate a pattern page onto heavy paper or card stock for each child. Make a sample craft to show the children.

WHAT TO DO

1. Introduce the lesson by telling the story from Mark 4:35-41. Ask, **When have you been in a really scary storm? Wouldn't it have been awesome to have Jesus say, "Stop" and then see the storm end? Jesus' followers were amazed that Jesus had power over nature. Only God's Son could have done that!**
2. Show the children the sample craft.
3. Distribute a pattern page to each child.
4. Say the memory verse.
5. Show how to cut out the circle and cut the spiral on the solid lines.
6. Have the children cut out the rectangle and fold it on the dashed lines.
7. Help the children tape a length of yarn to the top of the spiral and the bottom of the folded rectangle. Discuss the storms of life the children experience – illness, divorce, moving, etc. Say, **Jesus is always with us to help us.**

EXTRA TIME

Play "Simon Says" using "Jesus Said" instead.

Make a spinning spiral to remember that Jesus controls even the wind.

Even the wind and the waves obey him!

Mark 4:41

JESUS HEALS PETER'S MOTHER-IN-LAW

LUKE 4:38-39

MEMORY VERSE

So he bent over her and rebuked the fever, and it left her. She got up at once and began to wait on them.

~ Luke 4:39

WHAT YOU NEED

- page 62, duplicated
- crayons or markers
- scissors
- tape
- craft sticks

BEFORE CLASS

Duplicate a pattern page for each child. You will need four craft sticks per child. Make a sample craft to show the children.

WHAT TO DO

1. Introduce the lesson by having the children take turns reading Luke 4:38-39. Say, **This is a short story. But it shows us that Jesus took every opportunity to help others and to show He is God's Son. Think about what you were doing yesterday–how many times could you have done something to help or show love to someone?**
2. Show the children the sample craft.
3. Distribute a pattern page to each child.
4. Say the memory verse.
5. Have the children cut out the four puppets.
6. Show how to tape a craft stick to the back of each puppet.
7. Allow the children to color the puppets as time permits. Discuss ways each child can touch a life this week.

EXTRA TIME

Say, **Let's begin right here in our church to touch others' lives for Jesus. We don't have to perform a miracle and heal someone as Jesus did. But we can do little things to show love and kindness.** Do one or more of the following things in class: write thank-you's to the church staff, make gifts for elderly church members, share popcorn or cookies with another class or have an impromptu party and invite another class or parents.

Make puppets to tell this story.

So he bent over her and rebuked the fever, and it left her. She got up at once and began to wait on them.

~ Luke 4:39

Jesus Heals a Leper

Mark 1:40-45

MEMORY VERSE

Filled with compassion, Jesus reached out his hand and touched the man.

~ Mark 1:41

WHAT YOU NEED

- page 64, duplicated
- crayons or markers
- tape
- yarn

BEFORE CLASS

Duplicate a pattern page for each child.
Make a sample craft to show the children.

WHAT TO DO

1. Introduce the lesson by telling the story from Mark 1:40-45. Say, **Jesus had compassion on the sick man. How can we show compassion to others?** Suggest: be a helper, be a listener, provide food or clothing, be a good friend.
2. Show the children the sample craft.
3. Distribute a pattern page to each child.
4. Say the memory verse.
5. Have the children color the scene.
6. Show how to roll the page into a cylinder and tape at the seam.
7. Allow each child to cut two lengths of yarn.
8. Show how to tape one end of each length of yarn to the top of the windsock, then tie the other ends together to form a hanger.

EXTRA TIME

Have the children tape several 1-foot lengths of yarn to the bottom of the windsock. Have the children make some windsocks to share with nursing home residents. Plan a trip to deliver the windsocks as a class.

ake a windsock to remember
that Jesus had compassion on
a sick man.

Filled with compassion, Jesus reached out his hand and touched the man.

~ Mark 1:41

Jesus Heals a Paralytic
Matthew 9:1-8

WHAT YOU NEED

- page 66, duplicated
- pencils

BEFORE CLASS

Duplicate a pattern page for each child.

WHAT TO DO

1. Introduce the lesson by telling about the miracle found in Matthew 9:1-8. Have the children read verse 6 aloud. Say, **Why does Jesus say He said to the man, "Your sins are forgiven"?** (He wanted us to know that He is God's Son and has the authority to forgive sins.)
2. Distribute a pattern page to each child.
3. Say the memory verse.
4. Instruct the children to look in each of the listed verses to find the word with the missing letter and fill in that letter. Then they should write the five boxed letters on the blanks to find out what the paralytic and his friends had. Have someone read the word. Say, **Jesus saw that the men had great faith that Jesus would help their friend.**

EXTRA TIME

Allow the children to color the picture next to the puzzle.

riends carried a man to Jesus on a mat. Solve the word puzzle to find out what Jesus said the man and his friends had.

1. ___ orgiven (Matthew 9:2)

2. ___ eachers (Matthew 9:3)

3. ___ uthority (Matthew 9:6)

4. ___ ome (Matthew 9:7)

5. Pra___sed (Matthew 9:8)

___ ___ ___ ___ ___
1   3   5   2   4

The solution is on page 95.

JESUS WALKS ON WATER

JOHN 6:16-21

MEMORY VERSE

They saw Jesus...walking on the water.
~ John 6:19

WHAT YOU NEED

- page 68, duplicated
- crayons or markers
- scissors
- tape
- brown construction paper

BEFORE CLASS

Duplicate a pattern page for each child. Make a sample craft to show the children.

WHAT TO DO

1. Introduce the lesson by telling the children the story from John 6:16-21. Say, **The men were working hard to row the boat in the rough water. When they saw Jesus walking on the water, they were afraid. Then they let Jesus into the boat and He helped them. When we are working hard to get through a difficult time, Jesus is ready to help us.**
2. Show the children the sample craft.
3. Distribute a pattern page to each child.
4. Say the memory verse.
5. Have the children cut apart the page on the solid line.
6. Then have the children tape the flap to the edge so that the picture is facing forward. Show how to flip the flap back and forth to tell the story.
7. Have the children color the pictures as time allows.

EXTRA TIME

Have the children make a Pocket Promise to carry and remember Jesus' words from John 6:20 ("It is I...don't be afraid."). Have the children cut a paper rectangle, circle or square that is small enough to fit in their pocket. Tell the children to write the Scripture on the shape. If time permits, have the children make a Pocket Promise for a friend, too.

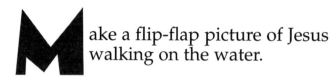

Make a flip-flap picture of Jesus walking on the water.

They saw Jesus...walking on the water.
~ John 6:19

JESUS PUTS A COIN IN A FISH
MATTHEW 17:24-27

MEMORY VERSE

Take the first fish you catch; open its mouth and you will find a four-drachma coin.

~ Matthew 17:27

WHAT YOU NEED

- page 70, duplicated
- construction paper
- crayons or markers
- scissors
- glue
- pennies

BEFORE CLASS

Duplicate a pattern page for each child. You will need one penny per child. Make a sample craft to show the children.

WHAT TO DO

1. Introduce the lesson by having the children take turns reading the story from Matthew 17:24-27. Say, **Although Jesus was the Son of God, He followed the rules of the times. What do you think Jesus would say about our rules today?**
2. Show the children the sample craft.
3. Distribute a pattern page to each child, and say the memory verse.
4. Have the children cut out the fish and show how to fold it on the dashed line.
5. Have the children glue the fish to a sheet of construction paper.
6. Show how to put some glue along the fold line, but not under the face portion of the fish so it can flap open.
7. Have the children glue a penny under the face portion of the fish.
8. Allow the students to color the fish. If time permits, provide glue sticks and glitter to decorate the fish.

EXTRA TIME

Play the Which Fish Game. Make several copies of the fish pattern or cut out a freehand fish. Tape a dime to the back of one fish. Tape a penny to the back of another fish. Place the fish on a table, coins down. Have the children take turns picking up a fish. If they get the one with a dime, they get a treat. Replace the fish after each turn and mix them up. Say, **Jesus put a coin in the mouth of one fish. He said to Peter, "Open the mouth of the first fish you catch and you will find a coin to pay the tax."**

ake a "hidden" coin fish.

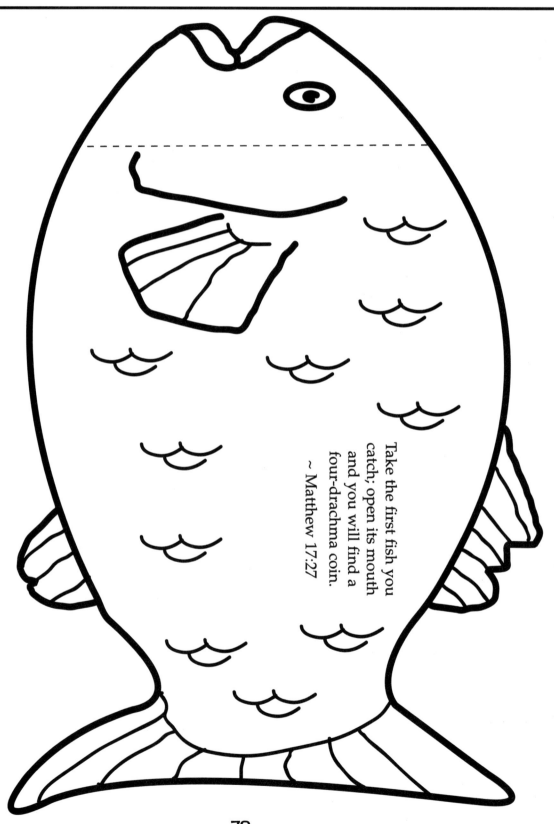

Take the first fish you catch; open its mouth and you will find a four-drachma coin.

~ Matthew 17:27

JESUS HELPS BLIND BARTIMAEUS TO SEE

MARK 10:46-52

MEMORY VERSE

"Go," said Jesus, "your faith has healed you."
~ Mark 10:52

WHAT YOU NEED

- page 72, duplicated
- crayons or markers
- scissors
- tape
- white paper
- yarn

BEFORE CLASS

Duplicate a pattern page for each child.
Make a sample craft to show the children.

WHAT TO DO

1. Introduce the lesson by telling the story from Mark 10:46-52. Say, **Bartimaeus had faith that Jesus could make him see. How can we have faith in Jesus today?**
2. Show the children the sample craft.
3. Distribute a pattern page to each child, and say the memory verse.
4. Have the children cut several 11-inch streamers from white paper.
5. Tell the children to write on each streamer something they are glad to be able to see with their eyes.
6. Have the children tape the streamers to the bottom edge of the Bartimaeus foldover.
7. Show how to tape a length of yarn to the top of each wind streamer.
8. Say, **Your wind streamer will remind you that Jesus gave Bartimaeus the gift of sight.**

EXTRA TIME

Play Blind Man's Trail. Arrange the children in a line. Have them hold hands with the person in front of and behind them. The first child in line is the leader. Have the rest of the children close their eyes. The leader should lead the class carefully through the room. Change leaders several times. Afterward, say, **That wasn't easy, was it? Let's take a moment and thank God for our gift of sight.**

Make a wind streamer to help remember this miracle.

"Go," said Jesus, "your faith has healed you."
~ Mark 10:52

"Go," said Jesus, "your faith has healed you."
~ Mark 10:52

Jesus Heals an Invalid at Bethesda

JOHN 5:1-9

MEMORY VERSE

At once the man was cured;
he picked up his mat and walked.

~ John 5:9

WHAT YOU NEED

- page 74, duplicated
- heavy white paper or card stock
- crayons or markers
- scissors

BEFORE CLASS

Duplicate a pattern page onto heavy white paper or card stock for each child. Make a sample craft to show the children.

WHAT TO DO

1. Introduce the lesson by telling the story from John 5:1-8. Say, **The man had been an invalid for 38 years. That's a long time! Yet the man was patient. He was very happy when Jesus made him well.**
2. Show the children the sample craft.
3. Distribute a pattern page to each child.
4. Say the memory verse.
5. Have the children cut the pop-up figures on the solid lines.
6. Have the children color the picture as time allows.
7. Show the children how to pop up the figures to tell the story: pop up Jesus when he walks by; pop up the invalid when Jesus heals him.

EXTRA TIME

Have the children sit on the floor with their legs tucked under their bodies. Have them sit while you're telling the story. Then suddenly say, **Get up and hurry to the other side of the room.** As they struggle to get moving after sitting on their legs, say, **The man in our lesson got up immediately and walked. Jesus made him completely well. The man didn't have to struggle because Jesus healed him.**

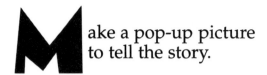

Make a pop-up picture
to tell the story.

At once the man was
cured; he picked up
his mat and walked.

~ John 5:9

JESUS HEALS A CENTURION'S SERVANT

MATTHEW 8:5-13

MEMORY VERSE

I tell you the truth, I have not found anyone in Israel with such great faith.

~ Matthew 8:10

I Have Faith

•

WHEN I'M AFRAID

WHAT YOU NEED

- page 76, duplicated
- pencils or markers
- scissors
- paper fasteners

BEFORE CLASS

Duplicate a pattern page for each child. You will need one paper fastener per child. Make a sample craft to show the children.

WHAT TO DO

1. Introduce the lesson by telling the story from Matthew 8:5-13. Say, **Many people saw Jesus do miracles. This man had faith that Jesus could heal him by only speaking. Jesus said this man had great faith!**
2. Show the children the sample craft.
3. Distribute a pattern page to each child.
4. Say the memory verse.
5. Have the children cut out the two circles, and cut out the window marked on the one circle.
6. Tell the children to place the window circle over the other one and push a paper fastener through both circles.
7. In the window, have the children write a situation when they have had to have faith (e.g., " When I'm afraid), then turn the wheel and write another situation and continue until the wheel is full.
8. As time allows, have the children decorate their faith wheels with markers, crayons or stickers.

EXTRA TIME

Write some life situations on slips of paper. Place the papers in a bowl. Have the children draw out a slip of paper. Discuss the best ways to have faith and handle the situations.

 ake a Faith Wheel to tell about
times when you have faith.

I tell you the truth, I have not
found anyone in Israel with
such great faith.
~ Matthew 8:10

I Have Faith

76

JESUS MAKES A WIDOW'S SON LIVE AGAIN

LUKE 7:11-16

MEMORY VERSE

They were all filled with awe and praised God.
~ Luke 7:16

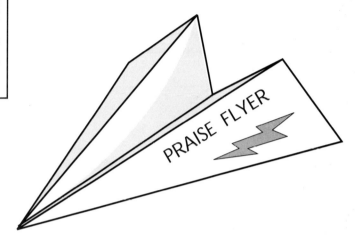

PRAISE FLYER

WHAT YOU NEED

- page 78, duplicated
- crayons or markers
- scissors

BEFORE CLASS

Duplicate a pattern page for each child. Make a sample craft to show the children.

WHAT TO DO

1. Introduce the lesson by telling the story from Luke 7:11-16. Say, **The people praised God for the wonderful miracles that Jesus did. We can praise God today for all the wonderful things He does in our lives.**
2. Show the children the sample craft.
3. Distribute a pattern page to each child.
4. Say the memory verse.
5. Have the children cut out the flyer on the solid lines, then fold it on the dashed lines as shown above.
6. Allow the children to color the flyer as time permits. Remind them to praise God for all He has done for them.

EXTRA TIME

Have some praise time with the children. Sing praise songs and let the students tell about things for which they praise God.

ake a praise flyer to remember that Jesus did wonderful miracles.

PRAISE FLYER

They were all filled with awe and praised God.
Luke 7:16

JESUS HEALS A DEMON-POSSESSED MAN

MARK 5:1-20

MEMORY VERSE

So the man went away and began to tell in the Decapolis how much Jesus had done for him.

~ Mark 5:20

WHAT YOU NEED

- page 80, duplicated
- clear transparency film
- permanent markers
- scissors
- fishing line
- hole reinforcement stickers

BEFORE CLASS

Duplicate a pattern page for each child on a sheet of clear transparency film. Make a sample craft to show the children.

WHAT TO DO

1. Introduce the lesson by telling the story from Mark 5:1-20. Say, **The man wanted to tell others what Jesus had done. God wants us to tell others what Jesus has done for us so they will believe in Him, too.**
2. Show the children the sample craft.
3. Distribute a pattern page to each child, and say the memory verse.
4. Have the children cut out the suncatcher from the transparency sheet.
5. Poke a hole in the top of each suncatcher.
6. Show how to place a paper reinforcement sticker on the front and back of the hole to keep the transparency from tearing.
7. Show how to thread a length of fishing line through the hole and tie at the top for a hanger.
8. Say, **When you hang your suncatcher in a window at home, you will be reminded that Jesus is Lord. He took away many demons from the man. Jesus is Lord of all.**

EXTRA TIME

Make a Jesus Is Lord bulletin board display. Provide magazines from which the children can cut pictures, and plain paper. Have the children cut out pictures from the magazines, or draw pictures, that show over what Jesus is Lord. Attach the pictures to your bulletin board with letters that spell out "Jesus Is Lord."

 nly Jesus, with the power of God, could take this legion of demons from a man. Make a suncatcher to tell that Jesus is Lord.

JESUS IS LORD

So the man went away and began to tell in the Decapolis how much Jesus had done for him.

~ Mark 5:20

Jesus Heals Jairus' Daughter
Matthew 9:18-26

MEMORY VERSE

*After the crowd had been put outside,
he went in and took the girl by the hand,
and she got up.*

~ Matthew 9:25

WHAT YOU NEED

- page 82, duplicated
- pencils

BEFORE CLASS

Duplicate a puzzle for each child.

WHAT TO DO

1. Introduce the lesson by telling the story from Matthew 9:18-26. Say, **The father showed great faith in Jesus. Let's solve a puzzle to show how this father showed his faith.**
2. Distribute a pattern page to each child.
3. Say the memory verse.
4. Instruct the children to fill in the blanks with the correct letters. They should use the code box to find the correct letters. Discuss with the children times we can show our faith in Jesus.

EXTRA TIME

Allow the children to color the picture, or turn the page over and write a story about a time when they showed faith in Jesus.

Solve the code puzzle to find out how this man showed his faith in Jesus in Matthew 9:18.

A1   C2   D3   E4   H5   I6

L7   M8   N9   O10   P11   R12

S13   T14   U15   V16   W17   Y18

___ ___ ___ ___   ___ ___ ___   ___ ___ ___
 2 10 8 4   1 9 3   11 15 14

___ ___ ___ ___   ___ ___ ___ ___   ___ ___
18 10 15 12   5 1 9 3   10 9

___ ___ ___,   ___ ___ ___   ___ ___ ___
 5 4 12   1 9 3   13 5 4

___ ___ ___ ___   ___ ___ ___ ___.
17 6 7 7   7 6 16 4

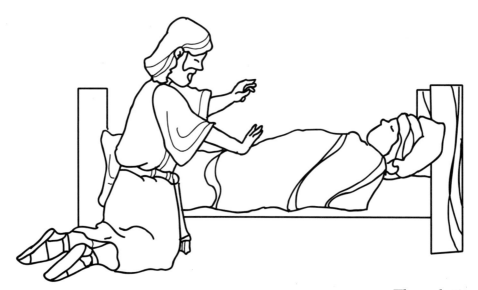

The solution is on page 95.

Jesus Heals a Sick Woman
Mark 5:25-34

WHAT YOU NEED

- page 84, duplicated
- pencils

BEFORE CLASS

Duplicate a puzzle for each child.

WHAT TO DO

1. Introduce the lesson by telling the story from Mark 5:25-34. Say, **The woman knew Jesus would help her if she could just get close enough to touch His clothes. We have faith that Jesus will care for us. We can get close to Jesus by reading the Bible, praying and other ways. Can you name some?**
2. Distribute a puzzle to each child.
3. Say the memory verse.
4. Encourage the children to solve the word-picture puzzle. Be available to help those who need help. Say, **God is happy when we have faith in Jesus like the woman did.**

EXTRA TIME

Play the Touch and Go Game. Say, **Let's play a game of Touch and Go to remember the great faith the woman had.** Play tag. Every time It tags another child, It should say, "Touch" and the tagged child should sit down. When all of the children have been tagged, It should say, "Go and be free." Choose another child to be It and play again as time allows.

Solve the puzzle to find out what Jesus said to the woman.

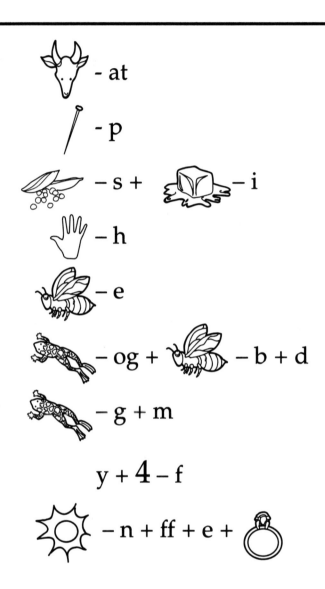

_____

_____

_____

The solution is on page 95.

84

JESUS HEALS 10 LEPERS

LUKE 17:11-19

MEMORY VERSE

One of them, when he saw he was healed, came back, praising God in a loud voice.

~ Luke 17:15

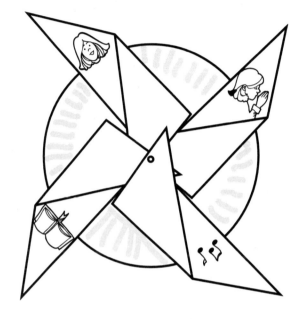

WHAT YOU NEED

- page 88, duplicated
- crayons or markers
- scissors
- paper fasteners
- paper plates

BEFORE CLASS

Duplicate a pattern page for each child. You will need one paper fastener and one 9" paper plate per child. Make a sample craft to show the children.

WHAT TO DO

1. Introduce the lesson by telling the story from Luke 17:11-19. Say, **We often forget to thank God for the things He does for us. This story is a reminder that we should praise God daily and thank Him for all of His wonderful care.**
2. Show the children the sample craft.
3. Distribute a pattern page to each child.
4. Say the memory verse.
5. Have the children cut out the pinwheel square then snip it inward on the solid lines.
6. Show how to fold in every other point toward the center.
7. Give each student a paper fastener to push through the center of the pinwheel and the center of a paper plate. Show how to fasten it on the back of the plate.
8. Allow the children to color the pinwheel as time allows. Remind the children to praise God and thank Him for all He does for us.

EXTRA TIME

Have the children write thank You letters or poems to God. Post the notes on a bulletin board with the memory verse.

Do you know how many lepers thanked Jesus? Make a praise pinwheel to remember that one man remembered to thank Jesus.

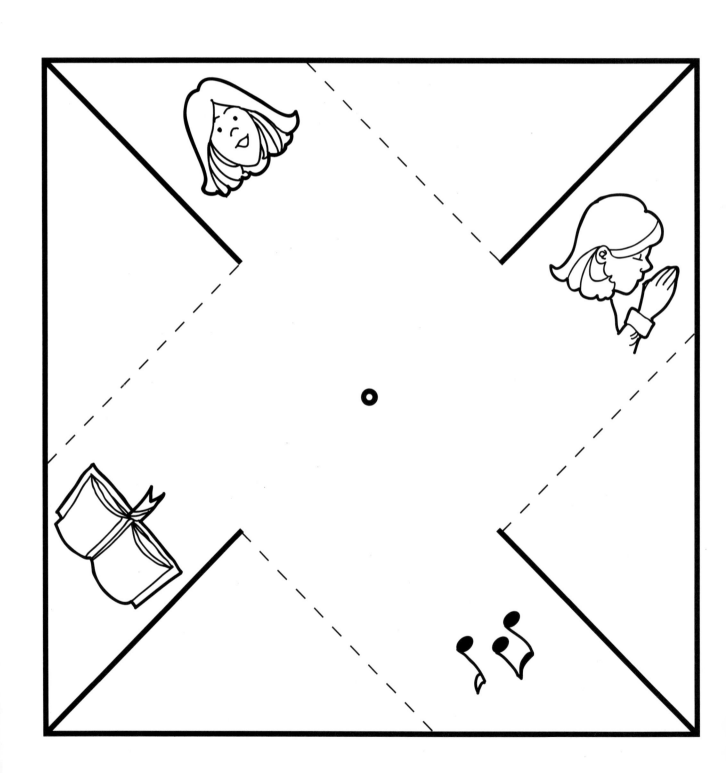

JESUS BRINGS LAZARUS BACK TO LIFE

JOHN 11:1-45

MEMORY VERSE

I am the resurrection and the life. He who believes in me will live, even though he dies.

~ John 11:25

WHAT YOU NEED

- page 90, duplicated
- crayons or markers
- pencils

BEFORE CLASS

Duplicate a pattern page for each child. Make a sample craft to show the children.

WHAT TO DO

1. Introduce the lesson by telling the story from John 11:1-45. Say, **Jesus reminds us that people who believe in Him will never die.** Ask, **Why did Jesus pray out loud?** (So the people would believe that God had sent Him.)
2. Show the children the sample craft.
3. Distribute a pattern page to each child.
4. Say the memory verse.
5. Have the children fold the page on the dashed lines.
6. Instruct the students to write the memory verse on the inside of the folding story. Have the children turn over the page and write a prayer or poem to thank Jesus for His power to conquer death.
7. Allow the children to color the picture as time permits.

EXTRA TIME

Provide robes and towels for costumes or let the children cut and color costumes from poster paper. Have the children act out the story for another class.

 ake a folding scene to remember that Jesus can conquer death.

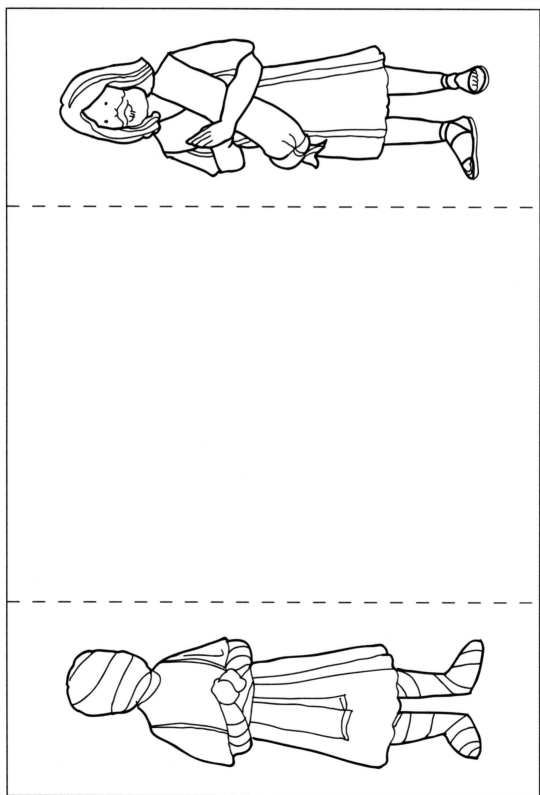

JESUS HEALED MANY PEOPLE
LUKE 4:40-42

MEMORY VERSE

The people brought to Jesus all who had various kinds of sickness, and laying his hands on each one, he healed them.

~ Luke 4:40

WHAT YOU NEED

- page 92, duplicated
- pencils or markers

BEFORE CLASS

Duplicate a puzzle for each child.

WHAT TO DO

1. Introduce the lesson by having the children take turns reading from Luke 4:40-42. Say, **More and more people needed Jesus. He could not get away because He was needed so much. Isn't it wonderful that we can talk to Jesus any time? We don't have to go a long way or wait in line. We can reach Him any time we want!**
2. Distribute a puzzle to each child.
3. Say the memory verse.
4. Tell the children to help each sick person find Jesus through the maze.

EXTRA TIME

Play the Real Life Maze Game. Map out a maze by placing yarn or rope on the floor. The maze should wind around the room through chairs and under a table. Have the children find their ways through the maze. At the end of the maze, be ready with Jesus stickers to give to the children. Say, **This maze is fun, but it took a long time to reach Jesus. We can talk to Jesus any time we want. Praise God!**

Five Minute

Help the sick people find Jesus so they may be healed.

The solution is on page 95.

JESUS IS THE SON OF GOD

HEBREWS 4:14-16

MEMORY VERSE

Let us hold firmly to the faith we profess.
~ Hebrews 4:14

WHAT YOU NEED

- page 94, duplicated
- crayons
- watercolor paint
- cups of water
- paint brushes or sponges

BEFORE CLASS

Duplicate a pattern page for each child. Use the cups of water to thin out the watercolor paint. Make a sample craft to show the children.

WHAT TO DO

1. Introduce the lesson by having the children take turns reading the Bible story from Hebrews 4:14-16. Say, **Jesus has been tempted to do all the things we are tempted to do. Can you name some of them?** Allow time for responses. Say, **Jesus understands our temptations. That's why we can have great faith in our Lord, Jesus Christ.**
2. Show the children the sample craft.
3. Distribute a pattern page to each child.
4. Say the memory verse.
5. Have the children color the picture of Jesus with crayons.
6. Help the students into paint smocks (men's old shirts work well).
7. Have the children use a brush or sponge to spread thinned watercolor paint over the picture. The crayon will resist the paint, and the background will look interesting with the painted surface. Say, **We can have great faith that Jesus will help us *resist* sin, just like the crayon *resisted* the paint.**

EXTRA TIME

Make a second copy of the Jesus picture for each child. Have the children copy all of Hebrews 4:14-16 on the back of the picture. Say, **These verses help us to remember that Jesus has already experienced things that we might experience in our lives. We can have faith that Jesus will always help us keep away from sin.**

Five Minute

Make a crayon resist picture
of God's wonderful Son.

PUZZLE ANSWERS

page 14
Neither do men pour new wine into old wineskins. If they do, the skins will burst, the wine will run out and the wineskins will be ruined. No, they pour new wine into new wineskins, and both are preserved.

page 48

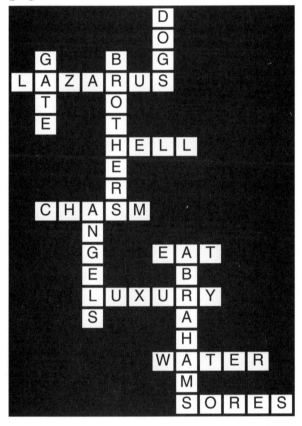

page 54

page 56

page 66
forgiven, teachers, authority, home, praised faith

page 82
Come and put your hand on her, and she will live.

page 84
Go in peace and be freed from your suffering.

page 92